Legislation Maze

# Fire

by Simon Ham

Series Editors: Sarah Lupton and Manos Stellakis

RIBA Publishing

Published by RIBA Publishing, 15 Bonhill Street, London EC2P 2EA

ISBN-13 978 1 85946 251 5

Stock Code 60749



British Library Cataloguing in Publications Data
A catalogue record for this book is available from the British Library.

Publisher: Steven Cross
Commissioning Editor: Matthew Thompson
Project Editor: Kelly Hallett
Designed by Philip Handley
Typeset by Academic + Technical, Bristol
Printed and bound by MPG, Cornwall



RIBA Publishing is part of RIBA Enterprises Ltd. www.ribaenterprises.com
Cover photograph: © Kim Steele/Getty Images

# Contents

# Legislation Maze series

This guide is in the Legislation Maze series, which comprises short, easy to use, topic-based guides to legislation for construction professionals (architects, engineers, surveyors, facilities managers, contractors) and students in construction-related fields. The series focuses on aspects of design and job management that are controlled by several statutory instruments and related codes and approved documents, and where assimilating these can be difficult and time-consuming in practice.

The series provides 'maps' to guide readers round the various relevant publications, with explanatory discussion as to their significance and relevance. It indicates which documents should be consulted in any given design context (for example, relating to building type, use, location, etc), and which are particularly relevant at each RIBA work stage. It provides practical, management-based guidance, pointing out the operational implications of the legislation (for example, when other consultants may need to be brought in), cross-linking the subject to different pieces of legislation and assessing the combined effect on aspects of design and job management. It expands on issues pinpointed in the Architect's Job Book, providing a bridge between these and existing technical publications.

This guide, *Fire*, comes at a time when there are substantial changes in the fire-related legislation. On the 1 October 2006, The Regulatory Reform (Fire Safety) Order 2005 came into force, replacing the Fire Precautions Act and over 70 pieces of legislation.

**Sarah Lupton and Manos Stellakis**
(Series editors)

# 1. Introduction

There has been legislation in respect of fire safety almost since man first started living and working in buildings. The Romans had rules defining distances between buildings in towns and tents in camps. A significant number of towns of timber framed buildings in Britain were destroyed by fire. While this afforded opportunities for the construction industry of the day, it was only after the Great Fire that legislation was brought in to control the form and construction for rebuilding buildings in London. Classical architectural forms came about partly as a consequence of a requirement for using non-combustible materials for the construction of walls and roofs.

Compliance with fire safety legislation can have a profound influence on the design of buildings and can result in a considerable amount of abortive effort if an architect fails to address and incorporate solutions as a design develops and is built.

There are essentially two ways of demonstrating compliance. The first is to follow the guidance in various approved government publications, national or international Standards or other credible guidance documents and publications, whether they have been officially approved or not. The second, generally accepted, way of demonstrating compliance is to develop an alternative fire engineering solution.

New buildings and controlled alterations and extensions in England and Wales are subject to the functional requirements of Part B in Schedule 1 of the Building Regulations. Once occupied most building types are subject to continuing control through **The Regulatory Reform (Fire Safety) Order 2005**.

**The Regulatory Reform (Fire Safety) Order 2005** was introduced with the aim of reducing the burdens on business that were caused by the existence of multiple, overlapping general fire safety regimes and consequently overlapping responsibilities of enforcing authorities. The order consolidates and rationalises a raft of earlier legislation and reduces the number of enforcing authorities. Responsibility for compliance falls on owners or managers of buildings within which people are employed. The impact of the legislation on architects is that they may be required by their clients to provide technical information on fire safety measures incorporated in their designs and also they may be commissioned to advise on the implementation of changes or improvements to existing buildings.

The aim of the reform was to simplify, rationalise and consolidate existing legislation and provide for a risk based approach to fire safety allowing more efficient effective enforcement by the enforcing authorities.

Fire safety legislation only addresses matters of life safety. The resulting fire safety measures often have some beneficial effect in terms of property protection. Although not directly subject to statutory control, a client's requirements in respect of property protection should always be established, probably in consultation with their insurers.

It must be appreciated that a significant amount of the legislation that controls fire safety as outlined in this book is new and even when the new legislation is built upon earlier legislation covering similar issues, all new legislation needs to bed down with the experience of use. It is only by being used that the full implications can be understood.

This book addresses the main pieces of legislation that cover fire safety in the design, use and management of buildings. It is not fully comprehensive and does not cover some of the more obscure references.

The book is concerned primarily with English and Welsh legislation and while there may be similar legislation in Scotland, Northern Ireland and to some extent in the Channel Islands and the Isle of Man, the form of the legislation and the method of enforcement in these areas may differ significantly.

Fire insurance and Insurer's requirements are often treated by clients as if they were quasi-legislation and therefore the role and status of insurance companies and their subsidiary organisations are also discussed.

Table 1.1 outlines key pieces of legislation, ordered to reflect their general significance and the Architects Plan of Work Stage at which they should be considered.

**Table 1.1** Principal current legislation affecting fire safety of buildings

| Legislation | Building Types | Notes | Architect's Plan of Work Stages | | | | | | | | | | | | |
|---|---|---|---|---|---|---|---|---|---|---|---|---|---|---|---|
| | | | A | B | C | D | E | F | G | H | I | J | K | L | M |
| Building and Buildings England and Wales Building Regulations 2000 | Apply generally unless specifically exempt as set out in Schedule 2, or work is not 'building work' as defined in Regulation 3 | Different Regulations apply in Scotland and Northern Ireland<br><br>Enforced by Local Authorities and Approved Inspectors who will consult with the Local Fire Authority, where appropriate | • | • | • | • | • | • | | | | • | • | | |
| The Regulatory Reform (Fire Safety) Order 2004 | Generally to all buildings in which people are employed | The legislation applies to employers' obligations repealing other fire safety legislation including the Fire Precautions Act 1971 and revoking other legislation including the Fire Precautions (Workplace) Regulations 1997 as amended in 1999 | | • | | | | | | | | | | • | |

**Table 1.1** Principal current legislation affecting fire safety of buildings

| Legislation | Building Types | Notes | Architect's Plan of Work Stages | | | | | | | | | | | | |
|---|---|---|---|---|---|---|---|---|---|---|---|---|---|---|---|
| | | | A | B | C | D | E | F | G | H | I | J | K | L | M |
| Local Building Acts excluding London Building Acts | Apply to specific types of buildings, mostly large storage buildings | Always check with the local authority whether there are local acts which apply to any proposed building work | | • | • | • | • | • | | | | | • | | |
| London Building Acts (Amendment) Act 1939 | Although much of the Act has been repealed, Section 20 still applies to certain large buildings in Inner London | When working in Inner London check if the building is covered. Approval may only be obtained from a local authority who will consult the LFEPA (London Fire and Emergency Planning Authority, which runs the London Fire Brigade) | | • | • | • | • | • | | | | | • | | |
| The Licensing Act 2003 | Applies to premises used for the sale of intoxicating liquor, the provision of public entertainment, theatre, cinema or the sale of hot food or drink after 11.00pm | Licensing conditions may affect the design of the building | | • | • | • | • | | | | | | | • | |
| The Construction (Health, Safety and Welfare) Regulations 1996 | Apply to construction sites | | | | | | | | | | | | • | • | |
| The Construction (Design and Management) Regulations 1994 | Apply to construction sites | | | • | • | • | • | | • | | | • | • | | |
| Housing Act 2004 | Applies to houses in multiple occupation or in any common parts of a building containing one or more flats | Enforced by the local housing authority who are obliged to consult with the fire and rescue authority for the area | | | | | | | | | | | • | • | |
| Fire Safety and Safety of Places of Sport Act | Sports facilities | Enforced by the local authority in conjunction with other relevant agencies including the police, fire and rescue and ambulance services | • | • | • | • | • | • | | | | | • | | |

# 2. Legislative framework

This chapter begins with an overview of the documentation that underpins the legal system and outlines the key legislation relating to fire safety in respect of buildings and construction. It is inevitable, in covering the generality of legislation and key guidance documentation, that some of the detail is lost; the reader is therefore always advised to check with the original source material.

European Directives are usually implemented in the United Kingdom through secondary legislation.

There is a plethora of documentation that an architect needs to have access to in order to fully grasp what is required from fire safety legislation. These documents are set out in Table 2.1.

**Table 2.1** Hierarchy of documentation for legislative control

| | |
|---|---|
| Primary Legislation | Acts of Parliament |
| Secondary Legislation | Orders, Regulations |
| Governmental, non-statutory supporting documents | Guidance Documents |
| Non-governmental, non-statutory relevant documents | International Standards, European Standards and British Standards |
| Documents that may be taken into consideration in determining compliance | Loss Prevention Certification Board (LPCB) Loss Prevention Standards, research papers, published articles |

Table 2.1 is best illustrated by using the Building Regulations as an example of how they apply to most buildings as shown in Table 2.2.

**Table 2.2** Application of the control structure to fire safety aspects of Building Regulations

| | |
|---|---|
| Acts of Parliament | The Building Act 1984 provides the Secretary of State with the power to make Building Regulations |
| Orders, Regulations | In the Building Regulations 2000, specific requirements are set out in the form of functional requirements in Schedule 1. Part B of Schedule 1 contains the functional requirements in respect of fire safety |
| Guidance Documents | The Secretary of State has issued guidance as to how these functional requirements may be complied with in the form of the non-statutory Approved Documents. Guidance on Fire Safety is provided in Approved Document B, Vols 1 & 2, and although this is not legally enforceable, it would provide a basis for resolving any dispute in respect of compliance with the functional requirements of Part B in Schedule 1. HTM 81 'Fire precautions in new hospitals' and BB 100 Designing and managing against the risk of fire in schools are examples of documents specifically referenced in Approved Document B as providing guidance in respect of these particular building types |
| International Standards, European Standards, British Standards | British Standards, European Standards and Building Research Establishment (BRE) Guides |
| Research papers, published articles, Loss Prevention Standards | Technical articles and published research papers may also be taken into account as above, but may be considered to carry less weight. Building Regulations are concerned with the health and safety of people, the primary concern of the Loss Prevention Certification Board (LPCB) Loss Prevention Standards is property protection, nevertheless their use might be considered relevant to demonstrating compliance with the Regulations |

As can be seen from Tables 2.1 and 2.2, Approved Documents offer practical guidance on satisfying the functional requirements, as set out in Schedule 1 of the Building Regulations. Following the guidance in Approved Documents is the most generally used way of demonstrating compliance with the Building Regulations. Because they are so widely used and available, Approved Documents are sometimes wrongly treated by both architects and building control officers as if they were Building Regulations. Table 2.3 should help to clarify their status.

**Table 2.3** Control Status

| | Function | Legislative status |
|---|---|---|
| The Building Act | Power to make Building Regulations | Primary legislation |
| ↓ | | |
| Building and Buildings England and Wales, The Building Regulations | These are the Building Regulations | Secondary legislation |
| Schedule 1 | The functional requirements | |
| ↑ | | |
| Approved Documents | The Secretary of State's interpretation as to how the functional requirements may be satisfied | Not legal documents, but are relevant to demonstrating compliance |
| | Approved documents include the relevant section of Schedule 1 | |

This documentation does not make easy reading but all architects should at least take the time to read through the general introduction and the introductory section to B1 in Approved Document B at least once.

Standards play an important role in describing what may be an acceptable means of demonstrating compliance with all fire safety legislation. It should be recognised that design standards in particular provide general guidance and may not be relevant to all circumstances. Product and test standards provide specifications which have to be met for them to be relevant. European Standards have exactly the same status as British Standards and their use is increasing, however at present the breadth of cover of British Standards is significantly greater than that of European Standards.

Local fire and rescue services play a significant role in most fire safety legislation either as enforcing authorities or by way of the legal requirement for them to be consulted as part of the process. In buildings such as entertainment complexes or hotels subject to control by a number of separate pieces of legislation different fire and rescue service officers may be responsible for providing responses to each piece of legislation separately and this advice may at times conflict. It is important to realise that consultation with the fire and rescue service as part of the Building Regulations approval process does not necessarily mean that the premises will be considered suitable for the issuing of a public entertainment license or a license to sell alcoholic beverages on the premises.

The following provides a brief description of legislation applicable to the design and construction process.

## Building Act 1984 (Chapter 55)

This is the legislation that grants the Secretary of State the powers to make Building Regulations, to relax or dispense with Building Regulations and to determine questions in respect of them.

Before making Building Regulations the Secretary of State is obliged to consult with the Building Regulations Advisory Committee and such other bodies as appear to him to be representative of the interests concerned. The RIBA is one such interest group.

**The Building Regulations 2000**
**Building and Buildings England and Wales**
**Statutory Instrument 2000 No. 2531**

There are a number of buildings and work to which the Building Regulations do not apply and these are set out in Schedule 2.

The Building Regulations apply to building work, material alterations and material changes of use (this is explained in more detail in Chapter 3 below).

The requirements of the Building Regulations are limited as set out in Part II, Paragraph 8:

> Parts A to K and N of Schedule 1 shall not require anything to be done except for the purposes of securing reasonable standards of health and safety for persons in or about buildings (and any others who may be affected by buildings, or matters connected with buildings).

Paragraph 16B set out requirements in respect of the need to provide fire safety information to the responsible person as set out in the Regulatory Reform (Fire Safety) Order 2005.

(1) This regulation applies where building work—
   (a) consists of or includes the erection or extension of a relevant building; or
   (b) is carried out in connection with a relevant change of use of a building,
   and Part B of Schedule 1 imposes a requirement in relation to the work.

(2) The person carrying out the work shall give fire safety information to the responsible person not later than the date of completion of the work, or the date of occupation of the building or extension, whichever is the earlier.

(3) In this regulation—

(a) 'fire safety information' means information relating to the design and construction of the building or extension, and the services, fittings and equipment provided in or in connection with the building or extension which will assist the responsible person to operate and maintain the building or extension with reasonable safety;

(b) a 'relevant building' is a building to which the Regulatory Reform (Fire Safety) Order 2005 applies, or will apply after the completion of building work;

(c) a 'relevant change of use' is a material change of use where, after the change of use takes place, the Regulatory Reform (Fire Safety) Order 2005 will apply, or continue to apply, to the building; and

(d) 'responsible person' has the meaning given by article 3 of the Regulatory Reform (Fire Safety) Order 2005.

The 'person carrying out the work' is not a defined term and is likely to be interpreted as being the builder or the client.

Fire safety requirements are included in Parts B and P of Schedule 1 of the Building Regulations. Part P1 requires that 'reasonable provision shall be made in the design, installation, inspection and testing of electrical installations in order to protect persons from fire or injury'. Approved Document P is primarily concerned with ensuring that controlled electrical work is carried out by a 'competent person' and includes no other specific guidance in respect of the fire safety of an electrical installation.

The Approved Document in support of Part B is divided into two volumes. Volume 1 is concerned with dwellinghouses and Volume 2 is concerned with buildings other than dwellinghouses. The documents contain very specific guidance on meeting the functional requirements. The individual functional requirements taken from Schedule 1 are repeated at the start of each section in both volumes of the Approved Document B:

- B1 Means of warning and escape.
- B2 Internal fire spread (linings).
- B3 Internal fire spread (structure).
- B4 External fire spread.
- B5 Access and facilities for the fire service.

The meaning of the term 'building work' is defined in the Building Regulations.

As far as fire safety is concerned, a material alteration occurs if the work, or any part of it, would at any stage result in a building not complying with the functional requirements of B1, B3, B4 and B5, where the building or a controlled service or fitting previously complied. Where a building or controlled service or fitting did not previously comply with the requirements of B1, B3, B4 and B5, a material alteration will also occur if the work makes the existing situation less satisfactory.

A material change of use will require that all parts of Part B are complied with irrespective of whether the building or a controlled service or fitting previously complied or not.

A material change of use occurs when a building is changed into a dwelling, or where the number of dwellings in a building is altered, or a flat is included where one did not previously exist. It will also occur when the building is changed into a hotel, a boarding house, an institution or a public building and where its use changes from one that was previously exempt.

## The Regulatory Reform (Fire Safety) Order 2005

Regulatory Reform, England and Wales
Statutory Instrument 2005 No. 1541

This order was not intended to introduce new requirements but is largely a consolidation of over 100 separate pieces of old legislation and, in particular, the old **Fire Precautions Act** and the **Fire Precautions (Workplace) Regulations**.

This legislation controls the use of non-domestic buildings after they have been occupied. A 'responsible person' will have the responsibility for carrying out and periodically reviewing a fire risk assessment of the premises, providing training to employees, keeping records and, where appropriate, liaising with other occupiers.

An essential part of any fire risk assessment will be a clear statement of the fire performance of the building, a description of all installed fire safety systems and a set of as fitted drawings showing these.

'Responsible person' as defined in paragraph 3 in the order as

- In a workplace, the employer if the workplace is to any extent under his control.
- The person in control of the premises in carrying on by him a trade, business or other undertaking.
- In the event that the person in control of the premises does not have control in connection with the carrying on by him a trade, business or other undertaking, the owner.

While the responsible person should be able to carry out some aspects of a fire risk assessment personally, there are likely to be other aspects (e.g. technical performance of the building construction) where they will be obliged to seek professional advice. This may prove to be a particular problem in older premises where original construction information has been lost.

Architects consulted on these matters should take care to avoid making absolute statements about the fire performance of existing construction. While a well constructed '9 inch' brick wall may reasonably be assessed as affording 60 minutes fire resistance, the likely performance of a timber door is extremely difficult to assess without physically taking it apart and establishing the provenance of the materials used in its construction.

The old **Fire Precautions Act** included a statutory bar preventing a fire and rescue service from requiring any work to be carried out above that required for compliance with Building Regulations. **The Regulatory Reform (Fire Safety) Order 2005** contains no similar bar. Issues may arise if an architect completes a building that complies with the requirements of the Building Regulations and the fire and rescue service subsequently require physical alterations to be made to the building after completion. In these circumstances the client may feel aggrieved with the architect.

The legislation is enforced by an enforcing authority (generally the fire and rescue service) in a number of ways, as detailed in Table 2.4.

**Table 2.4**

| Notice | Person served | Reason | Time for implementation | Appeal |
|---|---|---|---|---|
| Alterations Notice | The responsible person | If the enforcement authority is of the opinion that there is a serious risk to people on or in the vicinity of the premises this may include a schedule of steps to be taken to improve the situation | None stipulated | Technically it is possible to appeal through the magistrates' court but this should not be necessary |
| Enforcement Notice | The responsible person or any other person who has control to any extent in the building | If the enforcement authority is of the opinion that the requirements of the Order including any alterations notice, have not been met | As stated in the notice but not less than 28 days | Initially the magistrates' court with a right of appeal to the Crown Court<br><br>The affect of an appeal is to suspend the operation of the notice |
| Prohibition Notice | The responsible person or any other person who has control to any extent in the building | If the enforcement authority is of the opinion that the use of the premises will involve a risk to people on or in the vicinity of the premises so serious that the use of the premises ought to be prohibited or restricted | Immediate | Initially the magistrates' court with a right of appeal to the Crown Court<br><br>The affect of any appeal will not suspend the operation of the notice but may if the courts directs, suspend the giving of the direction within notice |

Where notices are served the advice of architects may well be sought in respect of the implementation of any building work that may be required.

Architects may also be requested to provide expert evidence in respect of any appeal but they should appreciate that greater weight may be given to evidence provided by a uniformed public servant, particularly in the magistrates' court.

## Local Acts

There are numerous local acts, which include requirements in respect of fire safety, including:

London Building Acts (Amendment) Act 1939 (c. xcvii)
East Ham Corporation Act 1957 (c. xxxvii)
Bournemouth Borough Council Act 1985 (c. v)
Greater Manchester Act 1981 (c. ix)
Isle of Wight Act 1980 (c. xv)
Plymouth City Council Act 1987 (c. iv)
Poole Borough Council Act 1986 (c. i)
Worcester City Council Act 1985 (c. xliii)
County of Avon Act 1982 (c. iv)
Berkshire Act 1986 (c. ii)
Cheshire County Council Act 1980 (c. xiii)
Clwyd County Council Act 1985 (c. xliv)
Cornwall County Council Act 1984 (c. xix)
Cumbria Act 1982 (c. xv)
Derbyshire Act 1981 (c. xxxiv)
Dyfed Act 1987 (c. xxiv)
East Sussex Act 1981 (c. xxv)
Hampshire Act 1983 (c. v)
Humberside Act 1982 (c. iii)
County of Kent Act 1981 (c. xviii)
County of Lancashire Act 1984 (c. xxi)
Leicestershire Act 1985 (c. xvii)
County of Merseyside Act 1980 (c. x)
County of South Glamorgan Act 1976 (c. xxxv)
South Yorkshire Act 1980 (c. xxxvii)
Staffordshire Act 1983 (c. xviii)
Tyne and Wear Act 1980 (c. xliii)
West Glamorgan Act 1987 (c. viii)
West Midlands County Council Act 1980 (c. xi)
West Yorkshire Act 1980 (c. xiv)

These acts apply to a range of issues, some minor, such as the requirement to provide fireman's switches on neon signs and others far more demanding, for example, requiring provision of sprinkler systems in large storage buildings.

Local building control departments should advise if there is a local act and what it covers. It is always advisable to ask. Private approved inspectors may lack knowledge in this respect.

Section 20 of the **London Building Acts (Amendment) Act 1939** applies to designated buildings in the inner London area and detailed guidance on compliance has been published by the London District Surveyors Association in their *Fire Safety Guide No. 1* – Section 20 Buildings, published in 1987.

## Licensing Act 2003 (Chapter 17)

This act requires certain premises used for the sale of intoxicating liquor, the provision of public entertainment (including theatre and cinema) or the sale of hot food or drink after 11.00pm to be licensed by the local licensing authority.

The licensing objectives are:

(a) the prevention of crime and disorder;
(b) public safety;
(c) the prevention of public nuisance; and
(d) the protection of children from harm.

Fire safety forms a significant part of any consideration of public safety. The licensing authority is obliged to consult the fire authority for the area in respect of their licensing policy and will consult the fire and rescue service in respect of the licensing of individual premises.

Licensing conditions may include limitations on the number of people using the premises and times when activities may take place.

Individual licensing authorities are responsible for publishing their licensing policy in the form of a licensing statement which is valid for and has to be renewed every three years.

Although licensing policies may be similar, as they are modelled on the same principles they will inevitably vary from one licensing authority to the next.

Where an architect is carrying out work in an existing building which has a premises license, or designing a building which will be used for an activity which will require a premises license, they should obtain a copy of the licensing statement to ascertain if it contains information pertinent to the design of the building.

It is advisable to obtain a provisional licensing statement under Section 29 where premises are being, or about to be, constructed for the purpose of being used for one or more licensable activities, or being altered or extended for that purpose.

It is unlikely that an architect will be required to make an application for a license but they may well be requested to provide drawings in support of an application and are advised to consult with the licensing authority in advance of a formal application being made.

## The Construction (Health, Safety and Welfare) Regulations 1996

These regulations require measures to be taken on construction sites which include preventing fires happening and making sure all people on construction sites, including any visitors, are protected if they do occur.

Measures that may be appropriate for consideration include the following:

| | |
|---|---|
| Fire prevention | Controlling people smoking and smoker's materials on the site |
| | Storing flammable materials properly |
| | Controlling any 'hot working' on the site, ensuring adequate protection of adjoining areas and checking after work has finished |
| | Ensuring that tar boilers are not left unattended |
| | Avoiding unnecessary stockpiling of combustible materials as they will be susceptible to arson and accidental ignition |
| | Adequately ventilating areas where volatile solvents and adhesives are used |
| | Avoiding burning waste and rubbish on site whenever possible |
| Raising the alarm | Establishing an appropriate means for raising an alarm and ensuring it is understood |
| Means of escape | Ensuring that there is an adequate number of escape routes and that they are kept available |
| Fire fighting | Ensuring that suitable fire fighting equipment is provided and that it is properly maintained |
| Emergency plans | Developing an emergency plan before commencement on site |
| | Clarifying responsibilities. Updating the plan, as necessary, as work proceeds |
| Information | Fire action notices should be displayed in areas where people congregate |

## The Construction (Design and Management) Regulations 1994

The CDM Regulations are aimed at improving the overall management and coordination of health, safety and welfare throughout construction projects to reduce accidents and ill health caused by the construction process. The regulations are likely to change as a consequence of a review and consultation exercise in 2005.

The coordinator and principle contractor will need to consider fire safety when preparing a health and safety plan for the construction.

## Housing Act 2004 (Chapter 34)

Although largely dealing with housing standards generally, this also controls licensing of houses in multiple occupation (HMOs).

In assessing conditions the local housing authority have the power to serve improvement notices and prohibition orders. Where a local housing authority considers that a fire hazard exists in an HMO or in any common parts of a building containing one or more flats, before taking any enforcement action, the authority must consult the fire and rescue authority for the area in which the HMO or building is situated.

HMOs are required to meet reasonable fire safety standards as a condition for licensing.

Compliance with fire safety requirements of Building Regulations should largely be sufficient to ensure that HMOs are suitable for licensing. Other measures not required under Building Regulations, such as the provision of fire extinguishers, are also likely to be required. Architects involved with this type of work should consult with the appropriate local housing authority department.

## The Fire Safety and Safety of Places of Sport Act 1987

The act requires safety certificates to be issued by the relevant local authority for regulated stands at sports grounds. No condition of a certificate should be such as to require a person to contravene any provision of **The Regulatory Reform (Fire Safety) Order 2005**.

Architects involved in this type of work should ensure that all the agencies involved in the certification process are properly consulted. Large fire authorities, for example, may have a number of different officers who could be involved in this process. For example, there could be an officer liaising with the building control department who is consulted as part of the building control procedure, a separate officer may be liaising on an alcohol license, a separate officer may be liaising on public entertainment licensing and yet another responsible for the ground safety certificate. They may all need to be separately consulted.

## Fire Insurance

Insurance is a regulated commercial business. The industry, through BRE Certification Limited which incorporates the Loss Prevention Certification Board, produces Loss Prevention Standards such as LPS 1039-5.1, 'Requirements and Testing Methods for Automatic Sprinklers'. Although the title of this document implies that it has legal status, in fact it has none.

It is often said by owners of commercial businesses that their insurers insist on certain measures such as sprinklers being incorporated into their buildings. This is not strictly true. The skill of insurance companies is to balance risk against premium and to spread their exposure to risk on the assumption that although claims will inevitably occur they are unlikely to occur simultaneously in all the risks covered. Insurers are unlikely to refuse to insure a risk; however, they will use their commercial judgement, largely based on experience, in setting a premium for the cover.

It makes commercial sense for insurers to offer to reduce their premiums in return for a property owner taking steps to reduce the risk. Complying with appropriate Loss Prevention Standards can be seen by Insurers as a means of reducing risk.

To maximise profits there is a significant benefit in insurers reducing their exposure to risk without significantly reducing the cost of premiums. However, insurance is a competitive market and insurers, like banks, benefit significantly from a reticence by people to shop around.

It is always sensible to advise clients to seek their insurers' views on any building development or work. While their views should always be taken into consideration they should not always be taken as binding. If their insurers are too demanding it may be sensible to suggest that clients investigate alternative providers. In theory, brokers should provide that service for clients but, as with insurance companies, some are better than others. There are about 600 insurance companies authorised to carry on general business in the UK. If UK companies appear complacent, advise the client to at least look into the possibility of seeking quotations from other parts of Europe or even other parts of the world.

**Table 3.1** Fire issues arising at different Work Stages

| Work Stage | Description | Fire issues to be considered |
|---|---|---|
| A | Appraisal | Is the location appropriate for the proposed building? |
| B | Strategic Briefing | Define which legislation is applicable and who is responsible for compliance and seeking consents |
| | | Establish who will be responsible for Building Regulations approval |
| | | Define property protection issues |
| | | Appoint a fire safety engineering consultant |
| | | Establish responsibility for fire risk assessment documentation |
| C | Preliminary Concept | In buildings where the fire safety provisions are critical to the form and planning of the building, preliminary meetings with enforcing authorities may provide the necessary comfort to enable the client to have the confidence to proceed |
| D | Final Concept | Development of initial fire safety strategy |
| | | Commission preliminary fire studies |
| E | Technical Design | Complete preparation of fire safety strategy |
| | | Finalise fire studies and fire engineering calculations |
| F | Construction Information | Apply for Building Regulations Approval |
| | | If necessary seek a determination |
| | | Develop a response to any conditions for consent |
| | | Consider the preparation of a preliminary fire risk assessment |
| | | Ensure that materials and equipment meet the required performance specification |
| | | Obtain copies of fire test documentation from manufacturers and/or suppliers. Check carefully to ensure that they are appropriate |
| | | Appraise other consultants inputs to ensure their design proposals are compatible with overall design objectives |
| G | Tender Documentation | With alterations or extensions, ensure that appropriate measures are incorporated to safeguard the means of escape of any existing occupants |
| | | Ensure that appropriate fire safety measures are in place on the construction site |
| H | Tender Action | Check prices appear appropriate for the works |
| J | Mobilisation | Fire safety of the construction site should be considered |
| | | Ensure that statutory notices are served prior to commencement of the works |
| K | Construction to hand-over | Respond to site inspections by statutory authorities |
| | | Ensure that variations to the works do not conflict with statutory consents |
| | | Ensure that equipment and materials conform with required standards |
| L | After hand-over | Ensure that any necessary certification of the premises is obtained |
| | | Provide as fitted drawings and sufficient documentation to enable the owners/occupiers to prepare a fire risk assessment of their premises |
| M | Feedback | Review fire safety design performance |

# 3. Work Stages: Preparation
## A–B Appraisal and Strategic Briefing

## A Appraisal

When looking at a site for development there are a number of fire safety issues that may be taken into account before planning permission is granted under the **Town and Country Planning Act 1990**. These issues include the following:

- The effect that a development may have on neighbouring premises. This could be important where a development involves a hazardous process or activity or generates noise late at night, in the case of licensed premises. It may be necessary or beneficial to 'woo' neighbours and elicit their support
- How close the development is to other risks, such as a development involving the storage of combustible materials next to an oil refinery or storage depot
- Availability of local water supplies for fire fighting purposes
- Whether local roads are suitable, to provide access for an appropriate fire fighting appliance

Some complex schemes may need to develop an early fire strategy as this can have a profound influence on the form of a building. Even less complicated schemes may need early consideration and even consultation for example where the viability of project depends on a solution that does not follow the guidance in Approved Document B.

## B Strategic Briefing

### Establish Legislation Applicable

Using Table 1.1 it should be possible to establish which legislation will be applicable to a particular project. It is important to establish who will be responsible for compliance and seeking consents and who will provide supporting documentation. While, for example, the client may take responsibility for an alcoholic beverage licence he may require the architect to provide any necessary drawings.

Not all building work requires Building Regulations approval and it is sensible to establish as part of the brief whether the work envisaged will require it. The following decision tree establishes the principles (see page 18).

### Establishing who will be responsible for building regulations approval

If Building Regulations approval is required consideration will need to be given to whether that approval will be sought through local authority Building Control or private approved inspectors. Whichever is selected they are both obliged to consult on relevant applications with the local fire and rescue service. While some private approved inspectors' fees may be lower than those of local authorities, which often have higher overheads, price should not be the only consideration. Local

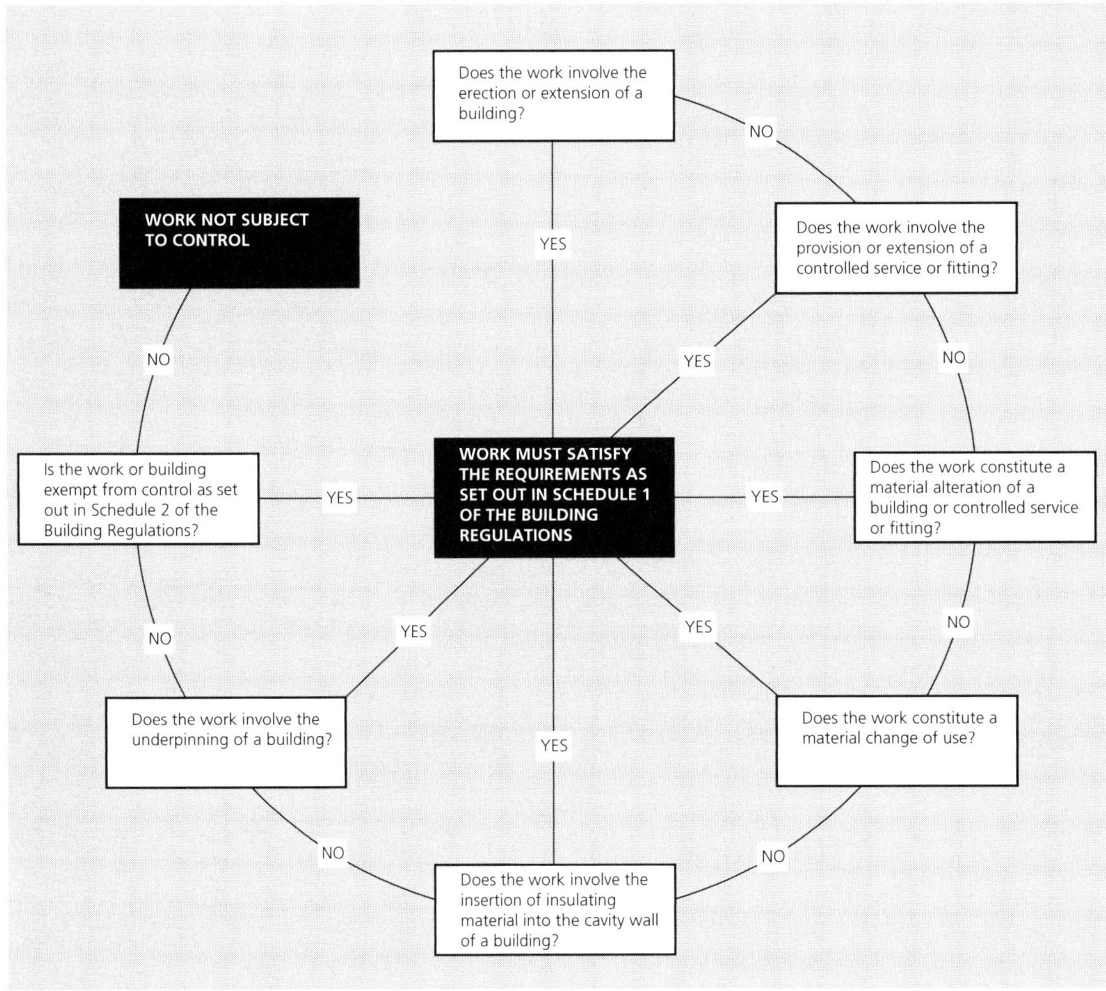


authorities are likely to have a well established relationship with the local fire and rescue service which can be helpful sometimes. There may be particular benefits in using a local authority where they have separate powers under the **Licensing Act 2003** or in London under Section 20 of the **London Building Acts (Amendment) Act 1939**.

### Property Protection

It will be sensible to establish at this stage any client requirements in respect of property protection. This should not only consider the building itself but also for example the implications of valuable items kept within the building or business critical equipment such as a computer with the only database of the clients business contacts stored on it.

The client should be encouraged to prepare a disaster plan involving decisions as to what should be saved first and how to mobilise and instigate programmes for salvaging water and fire damaged materials. This is particularly important in buildings containing priceless and irreplaceable artefacts such as museums.

Clients should be advised to consult on all aspects of property protection with their insurers or brokers.

### Appointment of a fire safety engineering consultant

Although a comparatively new discipline, architects and their clients are increasingly recognising the benefits of appointing a fire safety engineering consultant as part of the design team. The decision to appoint a fire safety engineering consultant on a project should be made on the basis of the following decision tree:

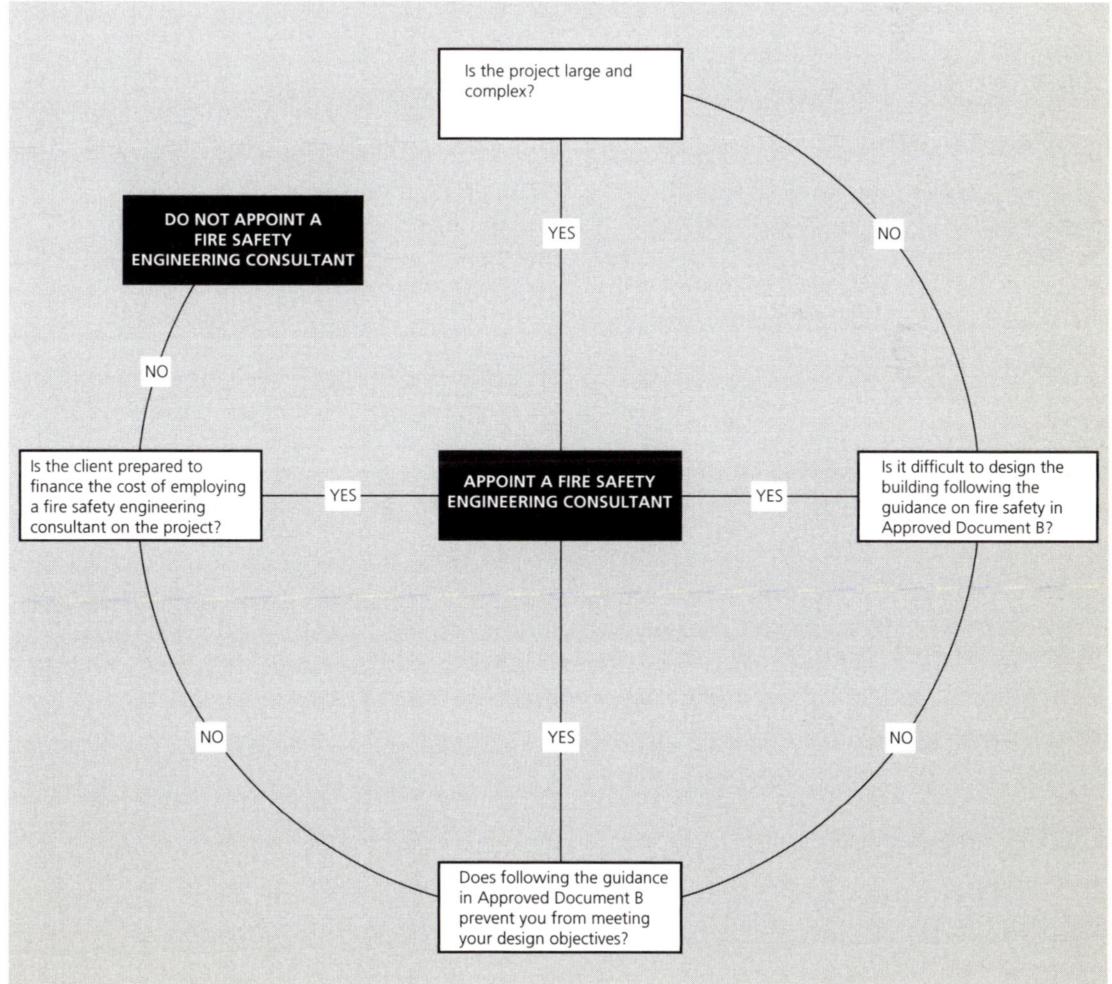

Anybody can set themselves up as a fire safety engineering consultant and the degree of expertise can vary considerably. While a retired fire officer may be able to assist with simple projects they are less likely to be able to handle more sophisticated approaches such as the use of computational fluid dynamic modelling. Although there are now established degree courses in fire engineering, the majority of leading practitioners have diversified into fire engineering from other disciplines. It is also advisable to select one by means of a personal recommendation or to look on the Institution of Fire Engineers website (*www.ife.org.uk*). It is also advisable to check that any fire safety engineering practice has adequate Professional Indemnity Insurance.

It should be recognised that insurance experience in respect of fire safety engineering is rather limited and it is difficult to obtain levels of cover in excess of £1 million pounds. While it may be possible to obtain cover on a project-by-project basis the premium for such cover is likely to exceed the fee for the work. The cost of the premium is therefore likely to be charged directly to the client.

**Responsibility for fire risk assessment documentation**

For all building types except for dwellings it is sensible to clarify in the design brief who will be responsible for the preparation of information to be used in conjunction with the preparation of any preliminary fire risk assessment prior to occupation of the completed building (see Chapter 7). This is likely to require some time and effort on behalf of all members of the design team, the cost of which may need to be taken into account in design briefs and fee negotiations.

While an architect may not be ultimately responsible for the preparation of a fire risk assessment, the client is likely to expect that the building is designed in such a way as to limit the risk to the eventual occupants of the building. The responsible person (see Appendix A) who will eventually prepare and periodically review the fire risk assessment is likely to be a business manager with a limited technical knowledge of building construction, fire systems and equipment. The responsible person will need to be provided with sufficient explanatory material in respect of the way the building has been designed and constructed to enable them to fulfil their role. Responsibility for providing such material will rest with the client who will undoubtedly expect that responsibility to be exercised through the architect and other professionals making up the design team.

## C Preliminary concept

**Preliminary consultation with the Building Control Authority and other enforcing bodies**

Although there is no legal obligation on the part of a Building Control Authority or approved inspector to offer to consult prior to an official application under the Building Regulations, where the proposed works are complicated or involve a fire engineering alternative approach it is sensible to do this. With a competitive market-place for building control this service is likely to be available and has the potential to save a lot of abortive design effort. Approving bodies may also be able to involve the fire and rescue service, entertainment licensing officers and officers responsible for licensing the sale or consumption of alcoholic beverages on the premises in any such early consultation. While early consultation may provide comfort for the client and the design team, any agreement reached at this stage will not be legally binding on an approving body and must be regarded as informal.

## D Final concept

**Development of initial fire safety strategy**

It is sensible to make a preliminary assessment as to how the building will meet the criteria for Building Regulations. This assessment should take the form of an initial fire safety strategy that provides the design team as a whole with a basis for progressing fire safety aspects of the design. It may be sensible to consult with enforcing bodies on the initial fire safety strategy.

Guidance on meeting the functional requirements of Schedule 1 of the Building Regulations is set out in a series of Approved Documents, Vols 1 & 2.

Approved Document B is concerned with fire safety. It is beneficial to establish the following basic set of parameters:

- The purpose group classification as described in both volumes of Approved Document B, Appendix D, table D1
- The height of the top floor above the ground
- The depth of the lowest basement storey
- The area of each floor
- The total floor area of the building
- The distance of the building from adjoining actual or notional boundaries

Using the above criteria the two volumes of the Approved Document sets out performance requirements as follows:

Volume 1 – Dwellinghouses

- Means of warning and escape, which includes:
  - fire detection and fire alarm systems
  - means of escape
  - work on existing houses
- Internal fire spread (linings), which includes:
  - classification of linings for walls and ceilings in terms of their surface flame spread characteristics and heat emission
- Internal fire spread (structure), which includes:
  - the fire resistance of load-bearing elements of the building's structure
  - compartment construction including the separation of garages
  - limitations on the extent of cavities
  - protection of openings and fire stopping
- External fire spread, which includes:
  - construction and performance of external walls and their surfaces
  - separation distance limitations from relevant and notional boundaries
  - construction and performance of roofs and their surfaces
- Access and facilities for the fire service, which includes:
  - fire fighting vehicle access to the building

Volume 2 – Buildings other than dwellinghouses

- Means of warning and escape, which includes:
  - fire alarm and fire detection systems
  - means of escape from flats
  - design for horizontal escape
  - design for vertical escape
  - general provisions
- Internal fire spread (linings), which includes:
  - classification of linings for walls and ceilings in terms of their surface flame spread characteristics and heat emission
- Internal fire spread (structure), which includes:
  - the fire resistance of load-bearing elements of the building's structure
  - compartment construction and size limitation
  - limitations on the extent of cavities
  - protection of openings and fire stopping
  - special provisions for car parks and shopping complexes
- External fire spread, which includes:
  - construction and performance of external walls and their surfaces
  - separation distance limitations from relevant and notional boundaries
  - construction and performance of roofs and their surfaces
- Access and facilities for the fire service, which includes:
  - fire mains and hydrants
  - fire fighting vehicle access to the building
  - access to the building for firefighting personnel

- provision of fire mains (wet or dry risers)
- criteria for the provision of fire fighting stairs and lifts
- where ventilation is necessary from basements

**Fire safety engineering**

Approved Document B, Volume 2 recognises that the prescriptive approach is not the only means of satisfying the functional requirements of the Building Regulations. It lists a number of alternative guidance documents setting out fire safety criteria for hospitals and shopping centres which, if followed, would be equally acceptable. In addition, it acknowledges that applying a fire safety engineering methodology can provide an alternative approach and 'may be the only practical way of achieving a satisfactory standard of fire safety in some large and complex buildings, and in buildings containing different uses, e.g. airport terminals'.

BS 7974: 2001, Application of fire safety engineering principals to the design of buildings, which is supported by a number of Published Documents, is one of a number of similar guidance documents on the subject of fire engineering. Three approaches for assessing the adequacy of a design are advocated:

(a) deterministic;
(b) probabilistic;
(c) comparative.

Although it is possible to develop a fire engineering solution from first principles using deterministic (using appropriate calculations and factors of safety) and probabilistic (statistically based) approaches, the majority of fire engineering solutions use the comparative approach. The ISO technical report BS ISO/TR 13387: Part 1: 1999, another of the guidance documents on fire safety engineering, describes how comparitive criteria should be used.

- The acceptability of a particular design may be evaluated by means of a comparison. The level of safety provided by alternative fire safety strategies can be compared with that achieved by the well established codes. This approach will generally involve deterministic and/or probabilistic techniques and therefore there is no clause entitled 'Comparative design'. The objective of a comparative study is simply to demonstrate that the building as designed, presents no greater risk to the occupants than a similar type of building that complies with a well established code
- For a comparative study it should not normally be necessary to include safety factors within the calculation procedures. Any inaccuracies in the assumptions made will have less effect upon the outcome than in a full probabilistic or deterministic study

Architects should avoid trying to buy their way out of problems they have created with complex technology. It should be recognised that the more sophisticated the technical solution the greater the chance of error. Smoke control systems for example may involve an array of engineering disciplines on the design side, a mechanical engineer to size the fans, an electrical engineer to supply primary and secondary power, a control systems engineer to programme the computer control system and a sprinkler engineer to limit the design fire size. These disciplines will be duplicated on the installation side and may be further duplicated within a contractor's design team. All the people involved have to communicate effectively with each other to achieve a satisfactory installation. The more people involved, the more opportunities for errors to occur. In general terms it is always sensible to work on the principle that the simpler a design solution is, the greater the chance it will be effective.

### Commission preliminary fire studies

Although forming part of an overall fire safety strategy it is sensible at an early stage to carry out preliminary fire safety studies on particular aspects of fire that may profoundly influence the form of the building, examples of which are included below:

- Where the project involves large numbers of people it may be sensible to prepare or commission preliminary escape evaluations to define the size and number of stairways and exits that will need to be provided
- If the design solution requires the use of a smoke control system, preliminary studies need to be carried out to establish whether this is best achieved by natural means or with mechanical assistance. Initial calculations should be prepared to establish the size of ventilation openings or the size and capacity of any smoke ventilation fans
- Where the building is located close to or on site boundaries it will be beneficial to establish the extent to which the external walls and their supporting structure need to be fire resistant by calculating the limits for unprotected areas
- In order to establish fire resistance periods it may be necessary to prepare an analysis of potential fire loading within the building
- In buildings incorporating unprotected or partially protected steelwork, the implications should be evaluated

# 5. Work Stages: Pre-Construction Period
## E–H Technical Design, Construction Information, Tender Documentation and Tender Action

## E Technical Design

### Complete Preparation of Fire Safety Strategy

As the design progresses the fire safety strategy will need to be refined. If the fire safety strategy is prepared in the form of a written document it should be completed prior to it being submitted in support of the application for Building Regulations approval.

Even at this stage, for more complex projects it may be sensible to consult with enforcing bodies on this fire safety strategy.

### Finalising Fire Studies and Fire Engineering Calculations

All fire studies and fire engineering calculations should be completed at this stage prior to being submitted in support of an application for Building Regulations approval.

## F Construction Information

### Application for Building Regulations Approval

In applying for Building Regulations approval it is beneficial to present any documentation, including drawings, in support of the application in a form that can be easily assimilated by the building control officer and the fire and rescue officers that they will consult.

The following should be considered:

- Prepare a dedicated set of drawings for this purpose. Remember there are no universally applied rules for the way in which drawings are presented. If it is possible to misinterpret what a line on a drawing represents it will be
- Avoid the inclusion of irrelevant information such as furniture unless it is necessary for the purpose of establishing travel distances
- Submit drawings at a scale that is legible but easily handled
- Highlight and/or include relevant information such as the basic set of parameters outlined in Work Stage D (Final Concept)

Consider also the implications of overcomplicating the drawings; for example, by marking each smoke detector position on the drawing rather than just including a note that an L1 fire alarm and detection system complying with BS 5839: Part 1 will be installed. It may be that the positions of detectors form an intrinsic part of the design in which case they should be marked on the drawings. However, if they do not, such detail included at this stage may compromise the approach of any design and installation contractor that implements the work.

Experience shows that more problems arise as a consequence of misreading or misunderstanding the information that has been presented than over technical issues.

### Determinations

If an application for Building Regulations approval is rejected by the approving body it is possible to appeal by seeking a determination. This process can take some time and requires a fee to be paid to the Secretary of State. Some practitioners apply to relax a regulation which harks back to the time when Building Regulations were prescriptive rather than functional.

The Building Act 1984, Section 30(1) contains provisions for the Secretary of State to determine questions that arise between a person who has carried out or proposes to carry out work and an enforcing building control authority. An application for a determination must be referred jointly by the applicant and the local authority to the Secretary of State, whose decision is final.

Paragraph (2) contains provision for an appeal to the High Court for an opinion in respect of questions of law arising from the determination which may influence the Secretary of State's final decision.

The Building Act 1984, Section 8 contains provisions for dispensing with or relaxing the requirements of Building Regulations. A referral to the Secretary of State on this basis is unlikely to be successful, as the regulations now take the form of functional requirements. Essentially, the requirements are that the building should be reasonably safe. Relaxing or dispensing with such requirements would suggest that it is reasonable in the circumstances for the building to be unsafe.

### Resolve any Conditions for Consent in any Building Regulations Approval

Building Regulation approvals increasingly contain a schedule of conditions. This is largely a consequence of local authorities endeavouring to meet service performance standards. These conditions cover items where the original application was unclear or where the enforcing authority considered that a particular issue was not fully addressed. Some of them can be extremely general such as satisfying the enforcing authority that the means of escape is adequate. It is important that each item in the schedule is fully addressed and agreed with the control authority as these items may be difficult and expensive to resolve when the works are nearing completion.

### Preliminary Fire Risk Assessment

There may be significant benefits to the client if the design team prepares a preliminary fire risk assessment to meet the requirements of The Regulatory Reform (Fire Safety) Order for the building prior to occupation. This work should be carried out in conjunction with the client and any management personnel for the building who might be available at this stage.

### Conformity with Standards

While most specifications refer to satisfying standard test criteria it may be necessary, and is certainly advisable, to obtain evidence of conformity from contractors and suppliers. This evidence may take the form of fire test reports, assessments and certificates. In reading these the specifier should ensure the circumstances in which products are used are adequately covered by the evidence presented. Approving bodies may also request copies of this evidence, particularly where new forms of construction or components are being used.

### Checking Consultants' Inputs

While ensuring that consultants' inputs meet the clients' brief and the overall design objectives is part of a continuous process commencing with the preliminary concept (Work Stage C), it is advisable at this stage to formally review these inputs.

## G Tender Documentation

### Alterations and Extensions of Existing Buildings

Where work is carried out in an existing building which remains in occupation, care needs to be taken that the tender documentation contains provisions for ensuring that the building in which the work takes place remains safe in the event of fire as required by The Regulatory Reform (Fire Safety) Order 2005. This may require the provision of special protection and temporary escape routes and will almost certainly require the fire risk assessment for the building to be amended while the work takes place.

### Site Fire Safety

Tender documentation should include reference to the need for the contractor and any subcontractors to be aware of their obligations and to make any necessary provisions under the Construction (Health, Safety and Welfare) Regulations 1996.

## H Tender Action

Ensure that any cost-cutting measures that arise from high tender prices do not compromise conformity with legislation. If necessary seek to amend any Building Regulations approval.

# 6. Work Stages: Construction J–K Mobilisation, Construction to Hand-over

## J Mobilisation

### Site Fire Safety

Check that contractor's proposals for fire safety conform with the **Construction (Health, Safety and Welfare) Regulations 1996**.

### Notices

The contractor is required to give two working days notice under Section 15(1) of the Building Regulations prior to the commencement of works on site.

## K Construction to Hand-over

### Site Inspections

Fire safety aspects of the construction may be subject to site inspection by the building control approving body. With fire engineered solutions care should be taken to ensure that requests on site from building inspectors are not implemented without consultation with the fire engineer.

It is essential that building inspectors are given an opportunity to visit the site prior to practical completion and are offered the opportunity to attend any commissioning and testing of systems and equipment.

### Variations

Any variations in the form of Architect's Instructions should be assessed for the requirements of Building Regulations. Where necessary the building approving body should be consulted.

### Conformity with Standards

Any alternative specifications proposed by the contractor, sub-contractors or suppliers should be subject to the same scrutiny previously outlined under Work Stage F.

## Prior to Practical Completion Handover and Occupation

Immediately prior to completion ensure that all necessary fire safety information is prepared for the 'person carrying out the work' to hand over to the responsible person carrying out a fire risk assessment for the building in use. They will require the following documentation:

- An as fitted drawing or set of drawings showing the fire safety provisions in the building. Architects preparing these drawings should recognise that managers are

unlikely to have facilities for storing large drawings. Ideally drawings should be A3 size to enable them to be kept folded in a file. Since most drawings are now available as CAD files it would also be sensible to either provide these drawings in this format to enable them to be updated when changes are made or ensure that the original architect's contact details are included in the fire risk assessment file. Architects should take steps to ensure that the copyright of drawings is not infringed. A check-list of relevant information to be incorporated on a fire drawing is included in Appendix B
- The total area for the building and a schedule of the area of the building on a floor by floor basis
- Documentation in respect of the fire strategy for the building, particularly if a fire engineering solution has been used as the means for satisfying the Building Regulations
- Full documentation on maintenance requirements for the construction and all fire safety systems. This should include service intervals and the need for service agreements
- A statement of the requirements and any assumptions that have been made in respect of the means of evacuation for disabled people
- A statement of any assumptions that have been made in respect of the way in which the building will be evacuated and/or managed

The 'person carrying out the work' will almost certainly require that the design team prepares and collates this documentation so that it can be handed over to the person responsible for managing the building once it is occupied. The handing over of fire safety information will be a condition for the issuing of a completion certificate by the building control approving body.

Immediately prior to handover seek a completion certificate from the building control approving body.

# 7. Work Stages: Use
## L–M After Hand-over, Feedback

## L After Hand-over

**Fire Safety once a building is occupied**

The fire and rescue service no longer certificates premises and will not necessarily carry out routine inspections. It will however participate in the process of safety certification for regulated stands at sports grounds under **The Fire Safety and Safety of Places of Sport Act 1987**.

Certain premises may be licensed by the local authority, who has an obligation to consult with the fire and rescue service. These include houses in multiple occupation under the Housing Act 2004, places of public entertainment and places where alcohol is sold under the **Licensing Act 2003**.

The Regulatory Reform (Fire Safety) Order 2005 requires that a responsible person in any workplace carries out and periodically reviews fire safety in the building in the form of a fire risk assessment. It requires that this assessment will have been carried out prior to occupation of the building. Any preliminary fire risk assessment prepared at the final design stage should be reviewed prior to occupation.

Architects may well have responsibility for their own workplaces and further details in respect of risk assessments are included in Appendix A.

## M Feedback

Fire safety design should be considered as part of any review of a building's performance in use.

# 8. Appendices

## A. Fire Risk Assessments

All employers within premises are required to carry out a fire risk assessment of their workplace and must regularly carry out a periodic review to keep it up to date.

As soon as is practical after carrying out the risk assessment or review, the responsible person must record the information if he or she employs five or more employees.

Employers must consider all employees and all other people who may be affected by a fire in the workplace. This includes making adequate provision for any disabled people with special needs who use or may be present on the premises.

The term 'fire risk' collectively describes both the risk of fire occurring and the risk to people in the event of fire.

The responsible person must identify the significant findings of the risk assessment and the details of anyone who might be especially at risk in the event of fire.

The responsible person must provide and maintain such fire precautions as are necessary to safeguard those who use the workplace.

The responsible person must provide information, instruction and training to employees about the fire precautions in the workplace.

The risk assessment will help the responsible person to decide the nature and extent of general fire precautions which they need to provide as well as fire precautions necessary to safeguard any process in which they are engaged.

There are six other legal duties:

- Where it is necessary to safeguard the safety of their employees, the responsible person must nominate people to undertake any special roles which are required under the emergency plan (they can nominate themselves for this purpose)
- The responsible person must consult their employees (or their elected representatives or appointed trade union safety representatives) about the nomination of people to carry out particular roles in connection with fire safety and about proposals for improving the fire precautions
- The responsible person must inform other employers who also have workplaces in the building of any significant risks they found which might affect the safety of their employees, and cooperate with them about the measures proposed to reduce/control those risks
- A person who is not an employer but has any control over premises which contain more than one workplace, is also responsible for ensuring that the requirements

of the fire regulations are complied with in those parts over which they have control.
- The responsible person must establish a suitable means of contacting the emergency services, and ensure that they can be called easily
- The law requires employees to co-operate with the responsible person to ensure the workplace is safe from fire and its effects, and not to do anything which will place themselves or other people at risk

The Department for Communities and Local Government have published a series of guidance documents, on carrying out risk assessments, primarily targeted at all employers, managers, occupiers and owners of premises.

## B. Fire Drawing Check List

Fire drawings will generally consist of a plan or set of plans, normally to scale. They should show the general arrangement within the premises including descriptions of the principal rooms, including room numbers where appropriate. While there are British (BS 1635) and International (ISO 6790) Standards for symbols on fire drawings, their use can be confusing for non-specialists. What is critical is that basic information is effectively communicated.

The following lists indicate some of the essential information that should be recorded depending on the complexity of the provision.

### Passive fire protection

- There should be a general statement on the drawings of the fire resistance of elements of the building's structure
- Fire resisting walls should be marked in such a way as to indicate their fire performance
- Fire doors should be marked together with their fire performance and closing mechanism

### Active fire protection

- Fire detection and alarm system:
    - detectors
        - heat
        - smoke
        - beam
    - sounders
    - call points
    - control panel
- Emergency lighting:
    - fittings
        - maintained
        - non-maintained
- Hose reels
- Fixed fire fighting mains:
    - dry riser
        - inlet position
        - outlet positions
    - wet riser
        - inlet position
        - pressure tank position and size
        - outlet positions

- Sprinkler system:
  - tank position and size
  - pump location
  - valve positions and method of operation
  - pipe runs and sizes
  - head positions, type and response time index
- Portable fire fighting equipment:
  - extinguishers – type, size and extinguishing medium
  - fire blankets
- Special measures:
  - smoke control systems
  - fire fighting stairways
  - fire fighting lifts

**Fire safety management**

- Fire safety signage including refuge indication signs
- Exit signs:
  - including illuminated exit signs forming part of the emergency lighting system
  - non-illuminated
- Procedure notices
- Risk identification signs
- The location of any high-risk areas, equipment or process that must be immediately shut down by staff on hearing the fire alarm
- The location of control rooms and fire staff posts
- Location of safe waiting areas for use by disabled people
- The location of the main electrical supply switch, the main water shut-off valve and, where appropriate, the main gas or oil shut-off valves
- The location of refuges and evacuation lifts for use by disabled people